Britt
Much joy To
you!

ME, WE and GLEE

How to have a great attitude, work as
a team, and keep your sense of humor

Nick Arnette

Me, We, and Glee:
How to have a great attitude, work as a team, and keep your sense of humor
Copyright ©2011 Nick Arnette
All rights reserved

Cover Design by Pine Hill Graphics
Interior Design by Pine Hill Graphics

Publisher's Cataloging-in-Publication Data
(Provided by Cassidy Cataloguing Services, Inc.)

Arnette, Nick.

    Me, we and glee : how to have a great attitude, work as a team, and
    keep your sense of humor / Nick Arnette. -- 1st ed. -- Los Angeles,
    CA : Nick Arnette, 2011.

        p. ; cm.
        ISBN: 978-0-615-45897-7
        Includes bibliographical references and index.

        1. Attitude (Psychology) 2. Stress management.
    3. Interpersonal relations. 4. Teams in the workplace--
    Psychological aspects. 5. Humor in the workplace--Psychological
    aspects. 6. Wit and humor--Psychological aspects. I. Title.

BF327 .A76 2011
158.1--dc22   1103

Printed in the United States of America.

To my
mom and dad.

Thanks for
the love!

Special Thanks

* To my really cool neighbors Myrna and Gail for being such fastidious and friendly proofreaders.
* To Stephanie Taylor for all the editing help.
* To Blake Joerger for telling me that I need to write a book.
* To Elwood Hale for being such a great friend and mentor.

Table of Contents

Introduction

Hey friends! Thanks for taking a look at what I affectionately call the *Me We Glee* book.

Do you tend to start a lot of books and not finish them because you just don't have the time to get through all of it? I've designed this book so you can probably read it in one or two sittings. There are lots of bullet pointed lists that you can refer back to as needed. I've even added some extra space so you can jot down a few ideas of your own.

I've divided the book into three sections:

1. *Me*—how your attitude impacts the course of your life.

2. *We*—teamwork: how to work well with others in a variety of situations.

3. *Glee*—the importance of humor in our lives. It's an ever-so-important component of the *Me* and *We* portions of life.

By the time you've finished the book, I hope you'll find that *Me*, *We*, and *Glee* are interrelated and vital components of daily life. If you have good *Me*, you'll have good *We*. And good *Glee* makes *Me* and *We* so much easier to maintain.

I'll keep this short, because to tell you the truth, I rarely read book introductions. So if you're anything like me, you're not even reading this part!

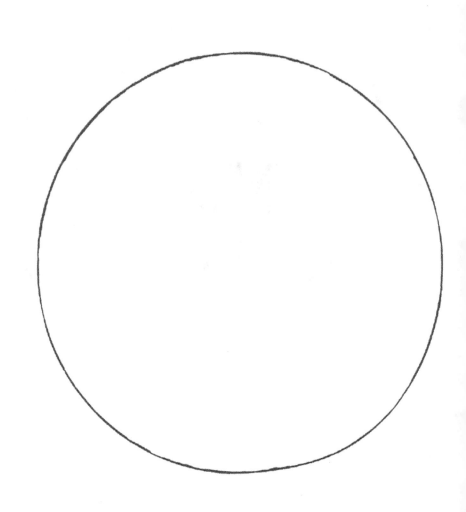

Being Good in the Moment

What's bugging you? Who's getting on your nerves? Too much to do, too little time? Your stressful commute to work? All the bad drivers on the road?

I live in Los Angeles, where traffic is so bad it would probably be more efficient to put my car in neutral and let the earth rotate than actually try to "drive" on the freeways.

Here's a chance to let out a little frustration. On the left is a blank circle. Your mission, should you choose to accept it, is to put one dot inside the circle for everything that's bugging you. Take your time; really think about it. Only you know what the dots represent, so have some fun with it!

How did that feel? Good, I hope. Now, take a close look at the circle. What else is inside the circle besides the dots? It's not a trick question. If your answer is "space," then you're a winner! If there's a lot more space than dots, then you're a double winner!! Actually, I've not yet met the person who has more dots than space.

If the dots represent what's bugging you, then the space represents what's not bugging you. It's all in the way we look at it. Yeah, I know, it's pretty basic, but most things in life are pretty basic.

Most people fail when they forget to use the "basics." Think about it: In golf, one of the fundamentals is to keep your head down. Still, even though I know that, I have a tendency to look up to see where the ball is going before I even hit it. The result is a bad shot and sometimes a lost golf ball. Keeping your eye on the ball is a must in every sport that has a ball in it. Still, from dropped passes to missed catches, many sports errors are made because we forget the basics.

Our biggest blunders usually occur "in the moment."

If you're in sales, maybe you didn't close the deal because you didn't ask for it. Or maybe you were talking so much that the client never had an opportunity to gather the information he or she needed. Again, it's the basics; we cannot stray from them if we want to succeed in our endeavors.

The same goes for our daily lives. Many of us have read about ways to reduce stress, to keep from getting angry, to manage our time better, etc. We may even have attended a seminar or two about it. Yet, when we blow it, it's because we forgot the basics.

Our biggest blunders usually occur "in the moment." Most of the time we do just fine. But let's add a little pressure to a situation. Someone says something offensive, or someone you were counting on doesn't come through, or someone repeats that annoying habit for the hundredth time—and we lose it. We might end up saying or doing something that we quickly regret, and we can't take it back. The damage is done.

One of my biggest annoyances is people who talk loudly on their cell phones in public. After one particularly tough gig, I boarded my flight home. Before we took off, the guy next to me was talking so loudly on his cell phone that I couldn't even hear the music I was listening to on my iPod. I couldn't wait for the plane to take off so he'd have to turn his phone off. When that time came, I turned to him and said, "Dude, way too loud on your cell phone." It was surreal. Was it *me* talking to him like that? I call myself "The Feel-Good Funny Guy," but in that moment, I was "The Make-You-Feel-Bad Knucklehead"! I offered my apologies for my errant comment, but the damage was already done.

He was crushed. He apologized and told me he hated his job, his phone was not working properly, and he was having a really bad day. I certainly did nothing to make it better. I acted like a jerk, and I knew it—and so did everyone else sitting near me on the plane.

I can honestly say I've never said anything brilliant when I was angry, nor have I done anything praiseworthy in a moment of anger. Have you?

Our prisons are full of people who have failed in the moment—people who have committed crimes of passion. They are average people who allowed their emotions get the best of them and did something that was out of character for them. They literally ruined their lives and possibly those

of others because they failed in the moment. Fortunately, you can't go to prison for telling someone he was talking too loudly on his cell phone!

When someone or something upsets you, ask yourself these three questions:

1. **What part of this can I do *nothing* about?**

   Like it or not, some things are completely out of your control. You can't control the weather, you can't stop time, and you can't control other people's attitudes and actions.

2. **What part of this can I do *something* about?**

   You can control—and are responsible for—your own attitudes and actions. How sad that many people have wrecked their careers or even their lives in an instance of uncontrolled anger. Again, they failed to remember the basics. They knew the proper way to handle their situation; they just didn't do it.

3. **How can I keep these thoughts going and get myself even more upset?**

   This sounds crazy, but it may be a good idea to think of all the ways you *shouldn't* react in a given situation, even though you might "feel" like it.

   For example, someone cuts you off in traffic. You might "feel" like responding by honking your horn incessantly and giving them the one-finger salute! You might even want to get ahead of the guy and cut him off, too, followed by driving well under the speed limit, just to make him angry and punish him some more.

What good can come out of this situation? Nothing. Two people are now angry, and more potential for mayhem exists. Even worse, have you ever honked at someone in traffic and they end up going to the same place you're going? How awkward is that?

Once you go through all the scenarios of what you shouldn't do (even though you might like to), you have a really good idea of how *not* to react to the particular circumstances.

Here's some space to put this concept into practice:

State the problem:

_____

_____

_____

Now ask yourself three questions:

1. What part of this can I do nothing about?

_____

_____

_____

_____

2. What part of this can I do something about?

_____

_____

_____

_____

3. How can I keep these thoughts going and get myself
even more upset? (This is where you really let yourself
go. Write down all the things you "feel" like doing to
take care of the problem—telling him or her off, leav-
ing without any notice, getting on top of your desk and
screaming, throwing a pie in his or her face, etc.).

_____

_____

_____

_____

_____

_____

_____

_____

_____

_____

Once you have completed step three, you'll have a whole list of ways *not* to respond to your problem. It would sure be fun to read some of your responses. If we put 'em all together, I bet we'd have the makings of the best sitcom of all time.

So really, what's the point of all this? Read on my friends. As the great philosopher Ricky Ricardo once said, "I've got some 'splainin' to do."

Active Vs. Reactive Mode

We have a choice of how we respond in a given situation. We humans operate in two modes: active and reactive.

In the reactive mode, we are operating out of instinct. It's our innate flight-or-fight mechanism. It comes in mighty handy when we need it.

Animals are always in a reactive mode. They only respond to how something else acts toward them.

I can remember a time when I rented a horse for a couple of hours. He was a big old horse named Prince. The stable hand said Prince was very nice, and I'd have no trouble with him at all—as long as I showed him who was boss. As soon as I was out of the corral and beyond sight of the stable Prince started acting up. He stopped dead (figuratively) in his tracks and wouldn't budge. I timidly gave him a "giddy-up" kick, only to have Prince turn around and try to bite me! I quickly surrendered and walked Prince back to the stable.

The stable hand asked me what was wrong. I sheepishly told her that Prince just wouldn't do what I wanted him to do. Well, she hopped on Prince and had him doing figure eights and a barrel race. I was so embarrassed. She said, "You just need to show him you're in charge."

Prince was operating in the reactive mode. He knew I was scared, and he reacted by not respecting my half-hearted commands. I also was operating in a reactive mode. I was afraid of Prince, and it affected everything else I was doing.

The stable hand, though, was completely in the active mode. She was in charge and had confidence in what she was doing. As a result, Prince was glad to follow because he was reacting to a competent equestrian.

When we are in the reactive mode our response is based on how someone acts toward us. *We're allowing another person to control us or the situation.*

In the active mode, our response is independent of the other person or the circumstances. We choose how we are going to both act and react. *We* are in charge.

> In the active mode, our response is independent of the other person or the circumstances.

My favorite active mode story involves my brother-in-law, Brian. He was the vice president of sales for a large home-builder. He was very good at his job and had proven himself to be one of the company's top-producing sales managers.

On his way to his daughter's eighth grade graduation, he was called back to the office with the bad news that his position had been eliminated. It wasn't personal. It was policy.

Brian is one of those people who is always happy. Now, the average American is in a bad mood 110 days a year. Only 2 percent are said to be in a good mood every day.[1]

Brian is one of the 2 percent.

He went through the entire weekend as if nothing was wrong; in his mind, nothing was. He didn't tell anyone about

---

1. Dianne Hales, *An Invitation to Health*, 6th edition, Cengage Learning, 2008, pp. 29-30.

losing his job until the weekend was over. We were all devastated by the news—everyone but Brian, that is. He went back to the office first thing Monday morning to clean out his desk. Eight hours later, he returned home. Why did it take him so long to clean out his desk, you ask? Because he spent the day writing thank-you notes to all the people he had worked with throughout his 11 years with the company—66 thank-you notes in all.

I saw him a week later, and he was wearing a sweatshirt with the company logo. I asked him why he'd still be wearing one of "their" shirts after being let go so unexpectedly.

Brian's response was a classic active mode response. He said, "Why wouldn't I wear it? They took great care of my family and me for 11 years. I wouldn't be where I am if it weren't for them. I'll always be grateful to them." He added, "I can't wait to find out what's in store for me next!"

You can probably guess that Brian had no trouble at all finding another job. As a matter of fact, the year he lost his job he ended up making the most money he ever had in his life. Art Linkletter said, "Things turn out best for the people who make the best out of the way things turn out."

What separates the novice from the professional is how they handle anxiety.

What separates the novice from the professional is how they handle anxiety. A novice isn't confident in his or her abilities and is more likely to fail in the moment. A pro, on the other hand, is at his or her best under pressure. That's when they shine; that's what made them great in the first place. Remember John Elway's "The Drive," where he marched his Denver Broncos football team 98 yards down the field to score with only minutes left in the 1987 AFC Championship game? How 'bout Brandi Chastain's winning kick in the 1999 Women's World Cup final game? Or Captain Chesley "Sully" Sullenberger's split-second decision to ditch the severely crippled US Airways flight 1549 into the Hudson River, saving the lives of all on board. These people were all great in the moment, and it greatly benefitted those with them.

You too can be brilliant in adversity by choosing to operate in the active mode. It's not always easy. You may still have some momentary failures, but the more you practice being in control of your thoughts, the more you'll be able to handle life's occasional setbacks like a pro.

When we are in the active mode, we are focused on the positive. (Remember the space and the dots?) Good thoughts in, good results out.

Our thoughts determine how we feel. How we feel affects our attitude. Our attitude influences our behavior. And our behavior molds our character. It all starts in the mind.

Healthy Thoughts = Healthy Body

What happens when we fill our minds with negative thoughts? I feel another illustration coming on...

I met some missionaries who were in Zambia during a terrible drought. There was only one source of water for miles around. Everyone and everything used that water for various purposes. Wildlife used the water—doing what animals do in and around water. People would bathe in it; others would carry the water back to town for cooking and drinking. Of course the water was making them sick due to all the contamination. But the people in the area didn't know what was making them sick. Fortunately, the missionaries showed them how to purify water and how to find other sources of clean water.

What those people were taking in was literally making them very sick. Our mind works the same way. If we fill it with negative thoughts, we produce unfavorable results. Have you ever said something you weren't expecting to say and then later asked yourself, "Where did *that* come from?" I rest my case.

Don't take my word for it. Check out what the experts say about it:

Only half of the heart disease in the United States can be explained by the traditional risk factors. The other half might

be caused by negative emotions such as depression, hostility, and anger.[2] For example, one study found that people who have "angry" personalities or are easily upset by stressful situations are more prone to heart disease.[3] Researchers have also found that positive emotions such as care, love, and appreciation increase immune antibodies and balance heart rhythms.[4] And a University of Pittsburgh study found that optimistic women outlived dour ones.[5] You don't need to be told that negative thinking is bad for you. We all know how it feels. It's not good. (So guys, if you want to be happy for the rest of your life, find an optimistic woman to be your wife!)

And a pessimistic outlook in the workplace will not only have negative effects on your ability to do your job, but it can also make you seriously ill. In the March/April 2003 issue of *Vibrant Life* magazine, Peggy Rynk writes:

2. Aggie Casey, Herbert Benson, Ann MacDonald, *Mind Your Heart: A Mind/Body Approach to Stress Management, Exercise, and Nutrition for Heart Health.* Simon and Shuster, 2004, p. 37.

3. Susan S. Lang, Richard B. Patt, *You Don't Have to Suffer: A Complete Guide to Relieving Cancer Pain for Patients and Their Families*, Oxford University Press, 1994, p. 221.

4. Bengt B. Arnetz, Rolf Ekman, *Stress in Health and Disease*, 1st edition, Wiley-VCH, 2006, p. 355.

5. Alice Park, "A Primer for Pessimists," *TIME*, March 26, 2009. http://www.time.com/time/magazine/article/0,9171,1887872,00.html accessed October 4, 2010.

In a study conducted at the University of Chicago on the effect of attitude on health, 200 telecommunication executives were observed as their companies downsized. The health of the executives who saw change as an opportunity for growth fared much better than those who saw it as a threat. Less than a third of the executives who had a positive attitude contracted a serious illness during or soon after the downsizing. But executives who saw downsizing as a personal threat had more than a 90 percent likelihood of becoming severely ill.[6]

Not only can unhealthy thoughts wreak havoc on our careers and our health, pessimistic thoughts often place all the power into the hands of the person, company, or situation that did us wrong.

Elwood Hale is my good friend and mentor. I described to him a disagreement I had with one of my best friends. I told him the whole story, probably even embellishing it to make my case stronger. All he said was, "That must have been very disappointing."

"If the solution to a problem rests on what someone else should be doing, control of your life has gone out of your hands..."

What, that's all? Really? I was looking for a little sympathy. Instead, Elwood followed with some very sage advice. He said, "If the solution to a problem rests on what someone else should be doing, control of your life has gone out of your hands, and into the hands of another human being."

6. Peggy Rynk, "The value of a healthy attitude: how faith, anger, humor, and boredom can affect your health," *Vibrant Life*, March-April 2003. http://find.galegroup.com/gtx/ start.do?prodId=ITOF&userGroupName=lapl accessed August 17, 2010.

In short, I was operating in a reactive mode. I saw myself as a victim. I was not in charge of the situation or my thoughts.

Elwood added another gem: "Don't let anyone determine what kind of day you're going to have or what kind of person you're going to be."

"Don't let anyone determine what kind of day you're going to have or what kind of person you're going to be."

So true! Many of the difficult people we've encountered through the years probably had no idea they were so irritating to us. Let's face it, they're usually clueless; that's why they're knuckleheads! Even if they were aware of their own cluelessness, chances are they probably weren't spending a lot of their free time thinking about you and how much they enjoyed getting under your skin. Why waste your valuable time and energy thinking or talking about them? Why would you want to give them so much power and control of your life? Focus on how you can be a better person and train yourself to focus on more positive things. It's not easy to do, but the alternative is literally a waste of time. On top of that, it's not good for you.

Happiness Vs. Joy

Do you want to be happy? Duh. Of course you do. Everyone wants to be happy. Being happy makes us feel good. That's what it's supposed to do.

Wanna hear something? I think happiness is highly overrated. "What? Are you kidding me?" you say.

Well, sort of. Yes, I love being happy. But the problem with happiness is that it doesn't last. By definition, the word "happy" is based on the word "happenstance." In other words, happiness is based on circumstances. Some of us get caught in the trap of thinking something is really wrong with us because we don't *feel* happy.

So some people do some pretty destructive things to make themselves "happy." They drink or do drugs or gamble excessively because it makes them happy—for a little while. Then that feeling goes away, and they want to feel happy again. If left unchecked, they wind up with an addiction because it takes more and more to make them feel happy.

I live in Los Angeles, a town where lots of rich and famous people live. I'm sure you've heard countless stories of people who had it all but were absolutely miserable. Consequently, their lives ended tragically. I'd venture to guess that if someone could ask them what they wanted out of life they'd say something like, "I just wanted to be happy."

If one of your goals in life is to live happily every after, you will probably wind up making yourself, and others around you, very *un*happy.

Joy is an internal sense of well-being, regardless of the circumstances.

Okay, now that I've bummed you out, don't despair. It's all good, I assure you. Instead of frustrating yourself by pursuing endless happiness, try hanging your hat on things that last. It's what's known as *joy*; it's an internal sense of well-being, regardless of the circumstances.

How do you get more joy? Focus on things that will last. That way when you are facing one of life's many challenges, you'll have something deep inside you to get you through.

Here are a few ways to boost your joy factor:

* **Take care of your body.**

    Eat right, get enough rest, and exercise. I bought a Nintendo Wii and use the Wii Fit exercise program. One day, my Wii Fit age was *20 years old!* (It made me more happy than joyful, because on most days, I'm much older.) Still, knowing that you are in good physical shape does a lot to keep your mind in the active mode.

* **Look after your spiritual needs.**

    Go to your place of worship. Join a small-group study at your church. Pray. It's always good to have someone to lean on who's bigger and stronger than you are.

* Volunteer.

One of the best ways to be fulfilled is to reach out to your fellow man. It gets the focus off you and onto others who need a helping hand. Teach someone to read. Clean a senior citizen's yard. Coach a little league sport. Go on a mission trip. Bring meals to the homebound. When you help others, you'll have a much brighter outlook on life. (Here's a prescription for a miserable day: Spend the entire day thinking of nothing but yourself and your problems.) Get outside yourself, and boost your joy factor and someone else's in the process.

* Be a family person.

If you have a family of your own, savor the time you have with them. Emphasize quality time together. Encourage and support one another. If you don't get along with your family, do your best to try to make things right. You'll get a lot of joy out of that.

If you don't have a family, "adopt" one.

If you're fortunate enough to come from a good family, be proactive and include someone who isn't as fortunate. Some of my favorite holiday memories are from times our family invited people who had no family to join us.

One thing is for sure: In times of need, one of the first places we turn to is our family. Do your best to maintain healthy relationships.

* Learn something.

Learning something new is always a good confidence booster. Learn to speak a new language, or take a class at your local community college. Knowledge is something anybody can get, and nobody can take it away from you.

* **Take on a hobby.**

Join a club with people who have similar interests. If you like to hike, join the Sierra Club. If you like to fly-fish, join Trout Unlimited. Having outside interests is a good stress-reducer as well as an effective joy-builder.

* **Expand your skills.**

In this economy, it's always good to make yourself as indispensable as you can. A good friend of mine is a financial troubleshooter for a large company. He was told he'd done so well that he had basically worked himself out of a job. He responded by learning how to use the complicated new accounting system the company had installed. Only a few knew how to use it, and now he's one of them! There is no more talk of laying him off.

Other ways of improving your skills might be attending conferences, joining associations in your industry, networking, or becoming an expert in your field. Be the first one to learn how to use the new equipment. Be good at finding quick answers to questions. Become the "go-to" guy or gal at your job. There's always a place for leaders and self-starters. It might as well be you!

If you're out of a job, become more skilled while you're looking. Use your time wisely. The time you spend worrying about not having a job can be spent learning skills to improve your chances of finding a new one.

* **Listen to positive things.**

Be careful what you listen to. I love music. I have about 12,000 songs on my iPod. I installed a program that found the words to most of my songs. Much to my surprise, some of my top-rated songs turned out to be very negative. Think of all that negativity stored in my subconscious! Some genres tend to be more negative than others. Instead, try listening to upbeat music and motivational or inspirational programs on the radio.

* **Watch what you watch.**

A lot of TV shows are essentially just guilty pleasures. Be careful. Don't let the skewed values displayed on many TV shows (especially reality TV) influence the way you think. Remember, garbage in, garbage out! At the very least, try to balance your TV watching with inspirational and educational programming.

* **Don't read into it.**

What we read can influence our thinking just as much as—if not even more than—what we watch on TV. If all we read is doom and gloom or gossip magazines, we can end up with a pretty pessimistic outlook on life. Everything we see and read gets stored in our subconscious mind. All of it. Take that into consideration when you're thinking about what you read (or watch). Try to balance your reading with something that is motivational or inspirational, especially at the beginning or the end of the day.

* Take it outside.

Being outside can be invigorating. Take a walk, do some gardening, smell some flowers, get a little sun. We get vitamin D from sunlight, and there are some valuable health benefits from it, such as an immune system boost, decreased risk of a battery of cancers (not skin cancer though, so don't get too much), protection from heart disease, and a decrease in joint and muscle pain. It also combats osteoporosis and weakening muscles.[7]

* Journal.

Get a notebook and write down all the good things in your life. You'll find that as time goes on your list will get longer and longer. You'll start focusing on the positive things in your life, and you'll be thankful for them. If you're having a hard time starting your list, go to www.youtube.com and search for "The Miniature Earth with Song." This short video breaks down what the world population would look like if there were only 100 people, using current statistics. After watching it, I assure you, you'll be able to list some good things in your journal.

* Be positive.

If you take on a positive, upbeat attitude, you'll find you start feeling that way too. It's the old "fake it 'til you make it." Also, when you're a positive person, you'll find you draw more like-minded people to you. Wanna

---

7. Monique Ryan, "The Missing Ingredient?" *Outside*, June 2010. http://outsideonline.com/ outside/bodywork/201006/vitamin-d-health-athletic-performance-tips.html accessed October 4, 2010.

hear a song about it? Listen
to "Change Your Mind"
by Sister Hazel. It's a good
theme song for active mode
thinking. You can't lose by
having a positive attitude!

* **Git 'er done.**

If you have something hanging over your head that
you're dreading—a project, something you need to tell
someone, etc.—just bite the bullet and do it. You'll
probably find it wasn't as bad as you thought it would
be. Even if it is, you'll be working toward solving a
problem that's robbing you of your joy. You'll have a
tremendous amount of self-satisfaction knowing that
you've accomplished something challenging.

* **Be good to yourself.**

If someone you deeply care for had a bad day, wouldn't
you want to do something nice to show how much you
value him or her? Sure you would. So remember to do
the same thing for yourself. Reward yourself for a hard
day's work or after completing a difficult task. It doesn't
have to be anything big or even cost any money. Just do
something that you enjoy doing.

Even taking a nap can do a lot to keep you feeling
good. More than 50 percent of Americans are sleep
deprived.[8] A 20-minute afternoon nap (right after

---

8. "A nap a day makes doctors okay, Stanford study finds," Physician Business Week,
November 21, 2006. http://www.proquest.com.ezproxy.lapl.org/ accessed August 23,
2010.

lunch is ideal) can increase your productivity and help you regain some of the sleep you lost the night before.[9]

* ## Look forward.

Be sure you have things to look forward to, both long- and short-term. Short-term ideas include meeting weekly with a group of friends, a golf game, a bowling league, a dance lesson, or going to church.

It's important to have some long-term things to look forward to as well, such as something you'd like to accomplish before a specified time, a special place you want to visit, the kids' graduation, grandchildren—the sky is the limit. Just be sure to have some!

We've all heard stories of people who survived dire circumstances mostly because they had something they were looking forward to. Having something to look forward to actually saved their lives.

Everybody needs something to do.
Everyone needs someone to love. Everybody needs something to hope for. And every- one needs something to believe in.

Lou Holtz

---

9. Arlene Weintraub, "Napping Your Way to the Top," *Business Week*, November 27, 2006. http://www.businessweek.com/magazine/content/06_48/b4011101.htm accessed October 4, 2010.

Okay, your turn. Write down a few things to increase your joy factor and keep you in the active mode of thinking.

_____

_____

_____

_____

_____

_____

_____

_____

_____

_____

_____

_____

_____

_____

_____

_____

Teamwork: What Is It?

Now that you've got your *Me* squared away, you'll be a natural when it comes to the *We* part. A person in the active mode anticipates and attends to the needs of others. In essence, it's teamwork. There's no "I" in teamwork, but the letters "WE" certainly are.

What is teamwork? How do we define it? Most would say something like "a group of people working together to accomplish a common purpose or goal." Would that be correct?

Let's take a little teamwork quiz.

Which of the following is an example of teamwork?

A. One person on the team does all the work, while everyone on the team gets the credit.

B. Everyone on the team does an equal amount of work, and everyone gets an equal amount of credit.

C. Everyone on the team does an equal amount of work, except one person, who does nothing, but that person gets all the credit.

D. Some people do all the work, the rest do nothing, but the entire team gets credit for it.

E. All of the above.

What did you guess as the correct answer? You probably chose: "B. Everyone on the team does an equal amount of work, and everyone gets an equal amount of credit." That is *a* correct answer, but it is not *the* correct answer. The right answer is: "E. All of the above." Yes, ALL of the above are correct.

How can they all be correct? Because teamwork is a very vague term. It needs to be defined so that everyone on the team will know what's expected of them. If the *team* doesn't know what teamwork is, how can they function as one? You've probably all been on a team in one of the aforementioned scenarios. It can be very frustrating and demoralizing if you're on the working end of the team while the rest, well…they just rest! But how can you say someone is not a team player if they don't know how a team is supposed to operate?

And teamwork doesn't just apply to the folks at the office. There are teams all around us: volunteer organizations, athletics, school clubs, etc. Your family is a team, too! Yes, even your family is a team, and just like your family, all teams are a little dysfunctional at times. The principles in this chapter will show you how to build great teams. As long as there is more than one person involved, there's a need for teamwork.

I used to teach high-risk children from the inner city of Los Angeles. The first thing I would do when I met them was shake their hands while I introduced myself. More often than not, I got a "noodly" handshake and no eye contact at all. As improbable as it seems, no one had ever taught them the proper way to shake hands. It didn't take long to teach them, and I reinforced it until it came naturally to them. The point

Teamwork is a very vague term. It needs to be defined so that everyone on the team will know what's expected of them.

is, don't take for granted what you think people may already know.

It takes a lot less time to sit down with your team and define exactly who and what your team is than to be enveloped in a team project with no clear direction or clear goals.

Teamwork does not come naturally. At some point every child will come down with "mine" syndrome. He will be holding something precious, and if you so much as pass within five feet of it, he'll grab it and cry out, "Mine, not yours." It doesn't matter how good his or her parents are, every child does it. Why? Because we want to take care of our own needs first. It's a natural instinct.

Furthermore, Americans don't place a lot of value on teamwork. What? We arguably have the best football, basketball, and baseball teams in the world. Take a moment to think of your favorite team in any sport and name all the players on the team. Can you do it? How about the starting

lineup? If you're like me, you can only name a few of the top players on the team. That's because we tend to place more value on individual achievements than collaborative efforts.

How about the performing arts? Think of your favorite band. You might be able to name all the band members. How about the people who mix the sound or run the lights? Can you name them? Aren't they all part of the team, too?

In America, we're taught, "Be the best *you* can be." We're not taught, "Let's all work together so everyone can share in the victory."

One summer, I taught English to a group of students from Indonesia. During recess, they were playing basketball, and I was impressed with their skills; however, I was more impressed by how they played as a team. They didn't take wild shots from far away. They passed the ball often. No single player dominated the game. When there was a hard foul and a player was knocked down, everyone stopped, helped the player up, then the game resumed as if nothing had happened. Here I was expecting to break up a fight, and instead I learned what teamwork might look like in another part of the world. Why did they respond as a team? Because that's the way they were taught, and they placed value on it.

Simply put, in our society teamwork is often ill-defined and undervalued. It is not ingrained in us as individuals or in our culture.

Nature has provided us an excellent example of teamwork in the California redwood trees. They are the tallest trees on earth; the tallest stands at more than 379 feet.

What's remarkable about these giant trees is their root system. Instead of a large taproot that grows down and deep into the soil, the redwood has myriad smaller roots that are relatively shallow. They grow laterally, intertwining with the roots of the other redwood trees. These very large and tall trees are literally holding each other up! They can't grow alone because they can't stand on their own. They hold on to each other so they can survive life's strong winds and storms.

The California redwoods have an advantage over us humans. They know how to function as a team without even being told. As for us, we need to communicate with one another. Herein lies the key: Good communication skills are the "root system" of teamwork. In my opinion, teamwork is synonymous with clear, well-defined communication.

From Their Mouths to Our Ears: Learning How to Communicate

Have you ever had a really really long argument with someone only to walk away and feel like they never heard you? Well, if you remember from the first section of this book, you can't control someone else's response. What you can do is learn good communication skills, increasing your chances of making difficult discussions go more smoothly in the future. By the way, I've never had a really really long argument, I was just using that as an example. Or, if I did, I don't remember hearing any of it!

So, what does it take to have effective communication skills? Let's study nuts and bolts of it.

* Maintain eye contact. Between 80 and 90 percent of all information absorbed by our brain is visual.[10]

* When listening, repeat in your mind what the other person is saying. It helps keep your mind from wandering and helps you avoid that deer-in-the-headlights look when they ask you a question.

---

10. Eric Jensen, *Brain-Based Learning: The New Paradigm of Teaching*, Corwin Press, 2008, p. 55.

* Be sure the other person is finished talking. Interrupting says, "What you're saying is not important. Shut up and listen to me."

* If you think you may be interrupting, say, "Were you finished with your thought?"

* Provide and ask for feedback. "What I heard you say was..." or, "I want to be sure I heard you correctly..." It instills camaraderie.

* "SILENT" and "LISTEN" contain the same letters. Coincidence? I don't think so. When you take time to listen, you convey the message, "I care, and you matter."

* Be alert for non-verbal messages such as body language and tone of voice. If a person is turning away from you or his or her voice is drifting off, that means it's time to wrap things up. Which brings me to my next point...

* Don't talk too much! Nothing is more annoying than someone who talks incessantly, mainly because they are only talking about themselves. Teamwork is impossible with one-way communication. If you're trying to sell something and you're doing all the talking, you're not selling anything. Never forget, "A fool is known by his multitude of words." You'll learn a lot more from listening than talking.

  (Quick self-test: If you continually find that people with whom you are eating are already done with their meals and you haven't even tasted yours, you're probably talking too much...or you know some exceptionally good listeners...or you only dine with really fast eaters!)

* Talk face to face as much as possible. It's easier to hear and understand when you see a person's facial

expressions and can read their lips. I have a lot of friends who speak English as their second language. When I'm with them face to face we communicate well, but on the phone we can barely understand each other. If at all possible, have important discussions in person, or try a visual medium such as Skype.

* Choose your words carefully. Try to use positive words as much as possible. One of my biggest pet peeves is when people ask me if I want some constructive criticism. I always answer with a very curt "no." It takes them completely off guard. They want to share their opinion so badly that they don't know what to say next. I guess most people answer "yes," but why? I must admit that this is one of my guilty pleasures, but really, who relishes criticism? A much better and more positive way to say the same thing is, "May I offer you a suggestion that might be helpful?" Now that's the kind of communication that builds teams.

Never take for granted that your team knows the essentials of effective communication.

Never take for granted that your team knows the essentials of effective communication. Actually, it's better to suspect that they don't. If you want to have a functioning team, you have to both show them and tell them how to communicate.

Pickin' a Mission

Okay, so now we've talked a little bit about how teams work. We've also thought about ways we can all communicate a little better, making it easier to put good teamwork into action. But what use is a team that doesn't know what it's supposed to do or where it's supposed to go? If you set out on a journey with no destination in mind, you will soon find yourself lost.

Your mission should be clear and concise.

The best place to start is with a mission statement. You can call it a goal, a slogan, or a motto. It just needs to state what you want to convey and accomplish. For our purposes, I'll refer to it as a mission statement.

Your mission should be clear and concise. There may be one overall mission statement for your business, such as, "Our company's mission is to provide quality products at affordable prices." Each department (sub-team) in turn would have its own mission statement, such as, "The goal of the Customer Service Department is to provide excellent service by treating our customers like family." You might even want to have mini mission statements for your meetings, such as,

"The goal of today's meeting is to choose a theme for our next event." The same idea works for your home, volunteer, or other activities. For example, a home mission statement could be, "Our family goal is to have quality family time."

Once you know your mission, you can discuss with your team how to achieve it. The family whose goal is quality time might agree to turn off the TV for an hour a night to do an activity of some kind together. Or, if you're super busy, it could be that you'll all eat dinner together with no interruptions or distractions at least once a week. It's your team, and it's your mission. Define it.

The sky is the limit when it comes to mission statements. The most important things are that it's clearly defined and that everyone on the team knows what it is. It's surprising to me that most people don't know their organization's mission statement. If you don't know where you're going on your mission, how are you ever going to get there? In addition to that, if you don't know where you're going, how will you know when you're there?

On the other hand, if you do know what your mission is, be it long-term or short-term, everything you do can be influenced by it—because you're on a mission!

When I was in first grade, my entire family went to Stapleton International Airport to see President Lyndon B. Johnson. Our mission was to see him and shake his hand.

We were on the tarmac waiting behind a thin rope as Air Force One pulled up near us. It seemed like hours, but finally, there he was, L.B.J. in all his presidential splendor. The president started going down the long line of people, shaking hands as he went. When he came near me, I was ecstatic. I was going to get to shake hands with the president! Well, he just passed right over my little first-grade hand. As a matter of fact, he didn't shake anyone's hand in my family, except for my mom's.

We were more than disappointed. My dad saw the disappointment on our young faces. My mom came up with a brilliant idea. She said, "Hey, I just shook the president's hand. So if I shake your hand, it will be just like shaking his hand." We all bought into it. Even my dad, although he might deny it. We all went home feeling like we'd accomplished our mission, thanks to my mom being a team player.

Sometimes accomplishing a mission requires a little flexibility, a little sensitivity, and a little imagination.

Take a little time to write a few mission statements for your life. The best way to get somewhere is to know where you want to go.

1. My mission at work:

_____

_____

_____

2. My mission at home:

_____

_____

_____

3. My volunteer/civic/spiritual mission(s):

_____

_____

_____

Making Teams and Team Meetings Effective

Whether you're on the marketing team at work or the fundraising committee at your child's school, meetings are a part of life. Since many missions start with team meetings, here are a few suggestions to ensure your valuable time is well spent:

* **State the purpose for your meeting before, during, and after the meeting.**

    If it's clearly stated, everything you do should revolve around that purpose.

* **Make sure everyone knows what you need to accomplish during your meeting, and focus only on that task.**

    If time remains, you can address other issues.

* **Place a high value on people's time.**

    Have a definite starting and ending time for your meeting, particularly if your team consists of volunteers. If your team meetings usually start late and end late, you're sending a message that your time is more valuable than theirs. Not good for team-building.

* **Resist the urge to retreat.**

A retreat is supposed to be a place to relax and rejuvenate. If you think a retreat is the time for an all day team meeting, think again. It's pretty vexing to sit in a meeting while looking out the window and watching people outside having a real retreat. The time spent planning and driving to and from the retreat can be more wisely spent by staying where you are. It frees up time and money for your team to have a genuine retreat to celebrate a mission accomplished!

* **Try to have balance.**

Your team may be filled with creative types who are idea rich and execution poor. Embrace those who are the worker bees. They are ultimately those on whom you can count to get things done. Be sure to include them in your discussions.

* **Use inclusive, engaging language.**

Ask questions such as, "What do you all think of this idea?" Or, "Let's hear from team members we haven't heard from yet."

* **Give everyone a chance to talk.**

If a few people dominate the conversation, other team members may lose interest and feel their ideas don't matter. The team may end up missing out on some very helpful ideas.

* **Set time limits before you ask open-ended questions.**

  Tell team members to answer in a minute or less (or whatever time limit you choose). Otherwise you might spend your entire meeting hearing someone babble on and on, which keeps you from accomplishing your mission.

* **Teach people how to behave at a meeting.**

  Don't assume that they already know. Remember, most people aren't naturally team players. Tell them it's important to give everyone a chance to talk, not to talk too much, not to interrupt, not to get up when someone is talking, etc. State this up front, then reinforce it during the meeting if needed.

* **Don't ridicule "stupid" questions.**

  Have you ever asked a question and were berated because you asked it? A typical response to your question would be something like, "You mean you didn't

know that?" If you want to close down communication and put an end to team building, make people afraid to speak up for fear of being scorned. Yes, sometimes the answers to some questions are so glaringly obvious it's almost all you can do not to say, "Duh!" But don't. Instead, answer in a polite, controlled tone and proceed with your meeting. Ignorance is not bliss on any team.

* Anticipate "flow killers."

Are there people on your team who continually ask off-track questions when your team is making plans? I lovingly refer to these people as "EGR"—Extra Grace Required! If you're the leader, try to meet with them before the meeting to reinforce the agenda and subject matter. Ask them—both before and after the meeting—if there's anything else they'd like to talk about so they'll still feel they are being heard.

* Get a wingman.

If you're leading a team, you need someone you can count on that's "got your six." This person is invaluable to you during meetings when someone's getting off track. Your wingman might offer a timely suggestion, such as, "Could we talk about this more after the meeting since our remaining time is limited?" Or, when you're in need of keeping the team together and focused during a project, they might say something like, "Hey, we're almost done, let's all chip in and help so we can finish." Your wingman is all-important to you and to your team. By the way, your wingman can also be a wingwoman!

* **Inventory your team members' strengths.**

   At your first team meeting, have each team member list his or her strengths and weaknesses, as well as any special skills they may have. Take a few minutes for each person to discuss what he or she listed. That way the entire team knows where its strengths lie, what it can do well, and areas where help may be needed.

* **Take one for the team.**

   Inevitably, there will be some tasks that no one will want to do. Jump in there and volunteer for them. It will speak volumes about your team spirit and your character, particularly if you're leading the team. If you want people to follow you, have an attitude of servitude.

* **Take into consideration that not everyone will see things the same way.**

   There are almost as many differing opinions as there are people. For instance, millennials—those born in the 1980s and 1990s—won't have the same life or work experiences as baby boomers. On the other hand, millennials can add lots of needed energy and optimism to your group because they aren't as likely to be jaded by past experiences. Use your team's differences to your full advantage. Think about it. Aren't horse races are based on differing opinions? Be sure to hear every member's viewpoint. You'll be backing the right horse.

* **Hold everyone on your team accountable.**

   Once you've decided on your mission and assigned your team members tasks to do, hold *everyone* on the team accountable for them. It does no good to spend a day making elaborate plans if there's not a strategy for carrying them out. Like my dad always told me, "Plan your work and work your plan."

* **Accept that not everyone will become a team player.**

This is where most of the conflict usually takes place. Have you ever been holding something heavy and other people are just standing around watching you struggle with it, not even offering to help? You think, how could they not know that I need help? You get angry. You start to fall into the reactive mode.

A possible resolution is to ask for help when you need it and praise the helper for pitching in. Some people just don't have a clue when it comes to teamwork, and you need to show them and tell them what it looks like.

Still, you can talk about teamwork until you're blue in the face (but try not to do that or you'll end up looking like a Smurf) and some people will not want to get with your team's program. There's a good chance they never will. Don't let that affect the rest of your

team. If you are required to keep these non-players on your team—if it's a work situation for example—give them specific individual assignments that don't require much collaboration. In time, if he or she sees the benefits of teamwork exhibited by other team members, they may want to hop on board. If they do, hooray! Just don't rely on it. These people rarely change their behavior. Think of their contribution as an added bonus that you weren't counting on. Who knows, "Lazy Larry" just might surprise your team sometime.

Remember, teamwork doesn't come naturally to most people.

Remember, teamwork doesn't come naturally to most people, and change is extremely difficult for some people. If they don't have to be on your team, find a nice way of giving them the boot! (This is much easier to do if it's in a non-work setting.) You don't want their negative attitude bringing the rest of the team down, and, believe me, it will if you allow it to continue.

Once I was leading a small team of five people. Four of the five would brainstorm new ideas, try new methods of communication, and talk about what we could do to improve our work. One of the five rarely participated in team discussions, took all suggestions as criticism, and literally frowned when anything was asked of him. After a while, some of the team members became resentful because this individual didn't contribute to the team no matter how much prompting we gave him. The atmosphere in the room became toxic when we were all together. He wasn't happy with the team concept, and the bad vibe was affecting our goal to become better at what we do. For you hipsters out there, "This dude was harshing our mellow." We went through the proper channels to remove him from the team. We found that our team was much more efficient and cohesive without him. Even though we were one member short, we had our team back, and we were better than ever.

* **Sometimes it's just not there.**

One person can ruin a team, even if he or she *wants* to be part of the team. It's like dating. Sometimes the chemistry just isn't there. Perhaps though, you can suggest another group that would be a better fit. Mention a particular strength you see in that person that would benefit another team. This is tricky. But just like dating, cut your losses and move on. No harm, no foul.

* **Pobody's Nerfect.**

Take it as a given that there will be problems on any team. The damage done in a moment of anger can shatter your team's morale and efficiency. Instead of losing your cool with other team members "in the moment," as we discussed in chapter one, set regularly scheduled times to get together with your team and discuss problems and challenges. When you allow time to pass, some problems seem to diminish on their own, and if not, well then, you can still talk about them at the meeting. Make it a rule that discussions about problems and concerns must be done in a civil manner and that breaking the rule will result in treating the team to lunch, dinner, or both if it gets way out of control!

* Write down any additional ideas you have about teams and team meetings here:

_____

_____

_____

_____

_____

_____

_____

_____

_____

_____

_____

_____

_____

_____

_____

Mission in Action

Now that you've planned your mission, you're off and running. At this point, everyone should know what to do and why they're doing it. If you're the team leader, be sure to reiterate the task at hand, so you're all on the same page. If you're going to be a team, act like one.

I once participated in an organized scavenger hunt that was designed to bring people together. We were split into two teams. Whichever team solved the riddles, collected the required items, and made it back to base first was the winner.

The two teams happened to collect the last item at the same time; the only task left was to go back to base. We were both waiting for a cab. I had an idea. I said, "Why don't we all win and just catch the Gold Line [a Los Angeles public rail service] back to base? That way, we'd save money, and we could all return together as two teams uniting as one."

The leader of the other team thought it was a great idea. Just then, a cab pulled up. One of my team members got in, and everyone followed. I did not want to leave the other team behind since we had an agreement. But someone on my team said, "Get in, hurry." I reluctantly hopped in and sheepishly apologized to the other team as we drove away.

We probably had the slowest cab driver in Los Angeles. He drove more slowly than any cab driver I've ever seen. We hit almost every traffic light.

Unknown to us, a driver of a nearby sightseeing van saw what had happened. He pulled up to the other team and said, "I saw your friends leave you behind. Do you want a ride?"

Teamwork:
A group of people working together to accomplish a common purpose or goal...

When we finally got back, the other team was getting out of the van and was first to reach the checkpoint. They had a better and faster driver.

I was glad we lost. We deserved to. We didn't communicate as a team. I learned a few valuable lessons about teamwork from it:

* **Integrity is of the utmost importance when working as a team.** If you agree as a team to do something, do it. Don't get caught up in the excitement of a situation and have a momentary failure. Think about how an errant decision—by even one team member who is off task—can affect the entire mission.

* **Resist the temptation to compete with other team members.** There is a time and a place to be competitive, but people on your team are not your competition.

* **Make every effort to create win/win situations.** For instance, I could have told the other team that we'd wait for them when we returned to base, and we'd all

walk in together. If I had said that, I'm sure they would have done the same thing for us.

Now, after this discussion, I think we have a new definition for teamwork: "A group of people working together to accomplish a common purpose or goal, in which all members are held mutually accountable for their contributions."

Individual commitment to a group effort — that is what makes a team work, a company work, a society work, a civilization work.

Vince Lombardi

Coming together is a beginning. Keeping together is progress. Working together is success.

Henry Ford

Stressed Out?

All right. You've got your *Me* and your *We* goin' on, but if you're under a lot of tension, it's hard to maintain. No doubt, people are stressed out.

According to the National Institute for Occupational Safety and Health, *three-fourths of employees believe that workers have more on-the-job stress than a generation ago.*[11] Next time an older person tells you how easy you "young whippersnappers" have it, tell 'em it ain't necessarily so!

Also, job stress is more strongly associated with health complaints than financial or family problems.[12] Look at the bright side, you might be so stressed out at work that you forget all about your personal and family problems. Okay, bad joke. Moving on.

The total health and productivity cost of worker stress to American business is estimated at $50 to $150 billion annually.[13] Dr. Herbert Benson of Harvard Medical School writes

11. "STRESS...At Work," National Institute for Health and Safety (NIOSH). http://www.cdc.gov/niosh/docs/99-101/ accessed September 11, 2010.

12. Ibid.

13. Steven L. Sauter, Lawrence R. Murphy, and Joseph J. Hurrell Jr., "Prevention of Work-Related Psychological Disorders: A National Strategy Proposed by the National Institute for Occupational Safety and Health (NIOSH)." *The American Psychologis t* 45, no. 10, October 1: 1146. http://www.proquest.com.ezproxy.lapl.org/ accessed September 11, 2010.

in his book *Timeless Healing* that 60 to 90 percent of all visits to doctors are stress-related.[14]

One study even suggests chronic *stress* also harms the brain, literally shrinking the hippocampus.[15] I don't know what a hippocampus is, but I don't think it's something we want to shrink. Too bad the hippocampus isn't located on the waistline! Hey, I looked it up. Evidently the hippocampus is thought to be the center of emotion, memory, and the autonomic nervous system. I told you it's something you don't want to shrink!

"A person who is resilient is less likely to suffer from the adverse effects of stress in the long run."

It doesn't matter if your stress is caused by your job, your lack of one, or too many time and family commitments. Stress doesn't make us feel good, and it's not good for us. Sonia Lupien, co-director of the Centre for Studies on Human Stress at the Douglas psychiatric hospital in Montreal, has some surprising news. Most of us think the opposite of stress is relaxation. Right? If I could just finish this project at work, or if I could just persuade the grandparents to take the kids for the weekend, then I could relax and I wouldn't be at my breaking point. But Lupien says the opposite of stress is *resiliency*. "A person who is resilient is less likely to suffer from the adverse effects of stress in the long run," she says.[16]

Did you highlight that? I think you could rephrase it by saying a person who stays in the *active* mode is less likely to

---

14. Stephen Devries, "Mind has effect on physical health," *Chicago Sun-Times*, February 28. http://www.proquest.com.ezproxy.lapl.org/ accessed September 11, 2010.

15. Aaron Derfel, "Deconstructing Stress," *The Gazette*, February 25, 2006. http://www.proquest.com.ezproxy.lapl.org/ accessed September 11, 2010.

16. Ibid.

suffer the adverse effects of stress. "Now how do I do *that*?" you ask. In this section we will learn how humor can help us stay in that active mode, and we will discuss easy ways to find humor in our daily lives.

Feel Good and Funny

Do you think humor is a luxury? Sure, you enjoy laughing and you like to spend time with friends whom you find funny. But in this busy world, you might think, *Humor is not a priority. I have more important things to do. I've got business meetings, Little League, and I need to make time for the gym, too. After that, if I'm not too tired, I'll try to have a laugh or two.*

You might want to rethink that. Laughter is as important to your health as going to the gym. And not only are the health benefits from laughter hard to beat, they are FREE!

Here's what the really smart guys and gals are saying about the health benefits of laughter.

Researchers at Wisconsin's Marquette University found that watching comedy clips actually improves memory.[17]

A study at the University of Maryland concludes that *laughter* causes blood vessels to expand and contract more easily. While stress constricts blood vessels by as much as 35 percent, *laughter* opens up blood vessels a whopping 22 percent more than when your body is at rest.[18]

---

17. Susan A. Smith, "TV Makes You Smarter," *Psychology Today*, July 1, 2004. http://www.psychologytoday.com/articles/200410/tv-makes-you-smarter accessed October 23, 2010.
18. Debra Williams, "Laughter is the best medicine," *Redlands Daily Facts*, October 7. http://www.proquest.com.ezproxy.lapl.org/ accessed September 2, 2010.

Laughing burns about 50 calories per hour.[19] Don't give up on the exercise, though, because it would take about six hours of laughing to burn off a cheeseburger. Kids laugh about four hundred times a day.[20] If you can manage to laugh just half as much as a child does throughout the day, you will give your heart a good workout.

Kids laugh about
four hundred
times a day.

"Laughing one hundred to two hundred times per day is the cardiovascular equivalent of rowing for ten minutes," says Dr. William F. Fry, associate professor of clinical psychiatry at Stanford University. "When something strikes you as funny, you laugh. And when you laugh, your body responds. You flex, then relax, 15 facial muscles plus dozens of others all over your body. Your pulse and respiration increase briefly, oxygenating your blood. And your brain experiences a decrease in pain perception, possibly associated with the production of pain-killing, pleasure-giving endorphins."[21]

Laughter also helps maintain a healthy immune system. It decreases stress hormones, lowers bad cholesterol, and raises good cholesterol.[22] Pardon my grammar, but when you laugh good, you feel good. Imagine the following conversation:

19. Ibid.

20. "Giggling? You've got to laugh." 2009. Daily Record, May 11, http://www.proquest.com.ezproxy.lapl.org/ (accessed September 7, 2010).

21. "Grin and bear it; Laughing does a body good," *The Patriot Ledger* [LIVING WELL Edition], September 28, 2005. http://www.proquest.com.ezproxy.lapl.org/ accessed September 11, 2010.

22. "Study finds body's response to repetitive laughter is similar to the effect of repetitive exercise," *NewsRx Health & Science*, May 16, 2010, p. 78. http://www.proquest.com.ezproxy.lapl.org/ accessed September 3, 2010.

Jeri: Hey Larry, you look great. What's your secret?

Larry: I've been laughing a lot...watching lots of comedy shows, reading funny books. You should try it. It's so much fun, and it makes me feel great! Best thing of all, it's free and has zero calories.

Jeri: I think I'll start laughing right now—about that ridiculous toupee you're wearing!

Norwegian scientists found that people with a sense of *humor* have a 30 percent higher probability of survival when severe disease strikes.[23] Like the old saying goes: He who laughs, lasts! When Sven and Inga tell you that your sense of humor might make you live longer, take notice.

---

23. Gayle Ritchie, "Death by numbers: Start counting the cost of your bad habits," *The Daily Mirror*, January 13, 2010. http://www.proquest.com.ezproxy.lapl.org/ accessed September 11, 2010.

Don't Be a Moody Dude

Laughter not only helps us stay healthy, it can help us get into the active mode. Maybe you know a "Gloomy Gus" or a "Debbie Downer"—a natural pessimist who's always in a bad mood. There definitely doesn't seem to be much humor in his or her life. Maybe you have been singing the blues lately yourself. But the good news is there may be ways we can help ourselves lift our own spirits.

Bad moods hit most of us an average of three out of every ten days.

Have you encountered a lot of moody people lately? Here's why. A University of Michigan study conducted by psychologist Randy Larsen showed that bad moods hit most of us an average of three out of every ten days. (Remember, staying in the active mode will help you minimize your bad moods!) An even scarier finding is that about 5 percent reported being in a bad mood four out of every five days.[24] Once you find out who these 5 percent are, give 'em lots of space! Better yet, RUN!!

So, don't feel bad if you occasionally need an attitude adjustment. According to Dr. Larsen, most of us do. Here

---

24. Dianne Hales, *An Invitation to Health*, 12th edition, Thomson Wadsworth, 2007, p. 51.

are a couple of studies that support the old adage "fake it 'til you make it."

The pen experiment: A control group held a pen in their hand and another group clenched a pen between their teeth, forcing a "smile." The pen clenchers rated cartoons as funnier than the control group. It's known as the facial feedback hypothesis.[25] Maybe there is something to "biting the bullet"!

The rubber band experiment: Researchers attached adhesive bandages connected with rubber bands to participants' faces and then raised and lowered their cheeks. The conclusion was that people may feel happy when their cheeks are lifted upward.[26] Go figure! I sure would love to have a picture of the people in that study. Wouldn't that be a hoot?

Even if you can't smile, there is still hope. Check out the Botox experiment: Participants were asked to read happy and sad statements before and then two weeks after Botox

25. *Fritz Strack*, Martin L. Leonard, Sabine Stepper, "Inhibiting and Facilitating Conditions of the Human Smile: A Nonobtrusive Test of the Facial Feedback Hypothesis," *Journal of Personality and Social Psychology*, May 1988, Vol. 54, Iss. 5, pp. 768-767.

26. Kazuo Mori, Hideko Mori. "Another Test of the Passive Facial Feedback Hypothesis: When Your Face Smiles, You Feel Happy," *Perceptual and Motor Skills*, 109, no. 1, (August), p. 76. http://www.proquest.com.ezproxy.lapl.org/ accessed September 2, 2010.

treatments. Great news for dermatologists: The world seemed less angry and sad after Botox treatments.[27]

Conclusion: If you don't want to smile, at least stop frowning. You'll be less angry and sad. In other words, you'll be chillin.'

So, the next time you're bummed out, put a pen or pencil (lengthwise, okay?) between your upper and lower teeth and see if you find yourself feeling happier. Try it. It really works. It's not a cure-all, but hey, it costs nothing to try. If you want to try the "not-frowning" experiment using Botox, you are completely on your own. If you want to save some money though, you can just stand outside on a cold, wintry day until your face freezes. Let me know how that works out for you!

Laughing is good for us, inside and out.

If you think that sounds like a lot of work and not terribly fun, the good news is that you really don't have to put a pen in your mouth or stick a needle in your face. Humor is an effective tool for reducing stress, improving productivity, and building teamwork—everywhere from the office to home. And laughing is good for us, inside and out. To tell you the truth, I think most of you already knew that without even reading about it. (At least now you have serious research to support your ideas.) You also know how it feels when humor is present, and how it feels when there's no humor at all. So now, let's find out how to put humor to use.

---

27. "Can blocking a frown keep bad feelings at bay?" *Surgery Litigation & Law Weekly,* University of Wisconsin-Madison, February 19, 2010, p. 1177. http://www.proquest.com.ezproxy.lapl.org/ accessed September 2, 2010.

Using Comedy to Flip the Equation

This is where *Glee* comes in. Nothing brings people together quite as easily as humor. Victor Borge said, "Laughter is the closest distance between two people." It's hard not to like someone after you've shared a laugh with him or her. It's a great door opener and barrier breaker. Why don't we use it more often?

In almost every joke there are two elements that cause us to laugh. The first is the element of surprise. Something unexpected happens; that's why it's funny. The second component is conflict. That's right, something that is disagreeable. Sitcoms are based on conflict; an everyday situation has gone awry. We can relate to the problem or situation, and we laugh about it.

What two factors contribute to our everyday problems like stress, anxiety, anger, frustration, impatience, worry, etc.? Did you guess the elements of surprise and conflict? If so, you're a winner! *The unexpected and conflict are the same two elements that trigger both laughter and anxiety.* We need humor to give us balance in our lives. You can get all worked up about something, or you can find the humor in it. You have a choice to be active or reactive. I know which one I'm choosing.

We've already discussed that kids laugh about four hundred times a day. What I haven't told you is this: The average adult laughs out loud about 15 times a day—on a *good* day.[28]

What happened to us adults? Why did we stop laughing so much? Well, it could be that as children our parents couldn't wait for us to learn how to talk. Once we learned to talk, they loved all the hilarious things we said as toddlers and preschoolers. Then about the age when we entered school, our parents kept telling us things like, "Sit down and shut up," "Wipe that smile off your face!" or "I'll give you something to laugh about."

> The average adult laughs out loud about 15 times a day—on a good day.

The older we get, the less we laugh—and the more it takes to make us laugh. We become more learned. It takes a whole lot more to surprise us. A baby will laugh when you hide your face behind your hand and say "peek-a-boo." Try that on an adult; the only reason they'd laugh is because they'd think you lost your mind!

As we mature, we start taking ourselves more seriously. We think we are supposed to act or look a certain way during home, work, or leisure time. We have a work face, a parent face, and a friend face. We have just a few "faces" that tell everyone who we are, and we're afraid of showing the world what we're really thinking. Again, let's take a look at children. They are very expressive with their faces; they are easy to read. We know what they are thinking just by looking at their faces. They don't worry what other people are thinking of them; they live "in the moment."

---

28. James L. Garnett, Alexander Kouzmin, *Handbook of Administrative Communication*, CRC Press, 1997, p. 232.

But when we're older, we have a harder and harder time being in the moment. Responsibilities pile up on us, and when something unexpectedly goes wrong, we can snap. But if we can use those elements of surprise and conflict to make ourselves laugh, we've won the battle. It's all in our perspective. Remember your circle with the dots from the very first chapter? There was more space than dots, right? So instead of letting surprise and conflict create stress and tension in your life, let's work on flipping that equation. Let's make those situations work for us, instead of the other way around.

If you've ever laughed while watching a sitcom, you definitely appreciate that comedy is based on conflict. You laugh at the situation the characters are in and you can identify with them. Believe me, most of what we are stressed out about today we'll be laughing about some day. Most of my comedy act is based on things that have gone wrong or didn't work out for me. Today's stresses are tomorrow's jokes. You might even say, comedy equals tragedy plus time.

For example, my worst gig: It was a Christmas party for a bunch of guys who hauled hay to farmers and ranchers. They were a rough bunch, and I was booked as the "clean" comedian, which is what the boss wanted. It wasn't what they wanted. They had an open bar before I went on, and

they were in no mood for listening to clean comedy. They didn't get any of my jokes at all. I tried all my best jokes, and there was absolutely no response. Within minutes there was a lot of talking, and they stopped paying attention. About five minutes into it, they were louder than me—even with my microphone turned all the way up! When I said, "Okay, I give up!" I got a standing ovation. They absolutely delighted in my failure. They jeered me all the way to my car. It wasn't funny at the time, but I guarantee you that I'm laughing about it now, even as I write this. Sometimes things are so bad, you just have to laugh to keep from crying. After some time passes, you just have to laugh…period.

Think of some things that have happened in your life that were a bummer at the time but now you have a good laugh when you share the story with your friends and family. Maybe it's the time you tore off the fender on your dad's first brand-new car, or the time you got your head stuck between the railings in the hallway, or the time you bounced a basketball on the piano keys to hear how loud it would be only to hear one of the keys break inside. I'm just using these as examples. I'm not saying they happened to me…or did they?

Write down a "tragedy time" event or two. You deserve a good laugh today.

_____

_____

_____

_____

_____

_____

_____

_____

_____

_____

_____

_____

_____

_____

_____

_____

_____

_____

Humor Works in the Workplace

Now maybe the one place you think humor is not appropriate is the workplace. They hired you to *work*, not goof off, right? But the workplace may be where humor is needed the most.

Chris Robert, a management professor at the University of Missouri-Columbia, says both sharing something funny and enjoying someone else's funny story can boost moods at the office. Maybe you already knew that, or are thinking to yourself, "Well, that makes sense." But it gets even better. Professor Robert's study indicates a strong link between mood and workplace performance and outcomes. That's right: *Funny makes for good business.* It's a new take on the colloquialism "funny business."[29] Note to self: Try to leave things I need done in the hands of happy people!

There's a strong link between mood and workplace performance and outcomes.

Perhaps one of the most notable examples of a company that incorporates humor into its business model is Southwest Airlines. I travel a lot with my work, and, as a passenger, I've consistently had good experiences with Southwest. The ticket

29. Tali Arbell, "This & That," *Pittsburgh Post-Gazette,* November 12, http://www.proquest.com.ezproxy.lapl.org/ accessed September 9, 2010.

agents, the pilots, and the flight attendants are typically cheery and often have something funny to say. I remember once on a bumpy landing the flight attendant got on the intercom and said, "Whoa, big fella." What were gasps turned into laughs because the flight attendant defused the situation with humor. On another trip we had to sit on the tarmac for more than an hour due to mechanical problems. The flight attendants led a trivia game until the plane was fixed. The prizes were peanuts (literally), but no one cared. The flight attendants turned an irksome situation into something fun.

Here are a few of my favorite jokes reportedly told by employees during Southwest flights:

"Hello, everyone. We have a first time flyer on board today—and it is also their 50th birthday!" After everybody cheers, the flight attendant continues, "Will everyone please wish the captain a happy birthday."

"Your seat cushions can be used for flotation. In the event of an emergency water landing, please take them with our compliments."

"As you exit the plane, please make sure to gather all of your belongings. Anything left behind will be distributed evenly among the flight attendants. Please do not leave children or spouses."

"Weather at our destination is 50 degrees with some broken clouds, but they'll try to have them fixed before we arrive."[30]

---

30. Howard Daughters, "In Flight Humor." http://www.funny2.com/inflight.htm accessed September 9, 2010.

Southwest employees use humor because the airline encourages it. They realize humor = happy employees = happy customers = good business.

This great attitude at Southwest Airlines started at the top, with Herb Kelleher, co-founder and former CEO of Southwest Airlines. He said Southwest looks for a sense of humor in the people they hire. During their interviews, prospective employees are asked to share how they've used their sense of humor to get out of embarrassing situations or to tell the funniest thing that's ever happened to them. Kelleher was asked if managers who encourage a sense of humor run the risk of not being taken seriously. He responded, "That comes from the old hierarchal theory of management, which says you have to show you're in charge by walking around acting like a brick all day. You don't persuade people you're serious by your demeanor. It's what you do that defines whether you're a leader or not, not how you appear."[31]

"It's what you do that defines whether you're a leader or not, not how you appear."

That's right. *It's what you do that counts, not how you appear.* So not only is humor good for workers, it can be a powerful leadership tool for managers, too. Some of our most loved leaders exhibited a wonderful sense of humor. Lady Nancy Astor said to former British Prime Minister Winston Churchill, "If you were my husband, I'd poison your tea." Churchill responded, "Nancy, if I were your husband, I'd drink it."

Former President Ronald Reagan, who had a terrific sense of humor, was known as "The Great Communicator." After

31. Donna Rosato. "Putting humor to work in the workplace. Guest CEO: Herb Kelleher of Southwest Airlines" *USA TODAY*, February 23. http://www.proquest.com.ezproxy.lapl.org/ accessed September 4, 2010.

being shot during an assassination attempt, he told his wife Nancy, "Honey, I forgot to duck!" This put the entire nation at ease. People's response was, "Ron still has his *wits* about him. He is still in control of the situation." We had a sense that everything was going to be okay.

The person in charge sets the tone for everyone else. If the boss laughs, everyone laughs. If you're the boss, don't be afraid to poke a little fun at yourself once in a while. It generates trust, builds rapport, and fosters an attitude of teamwork. Using a sense of humor to manage and lead people is a great way to diminish the "us versus them" gap in the workplace. Just make sure you use it correctly. "How do I do that?" you ask? Well, that's what we're going to talk about next.

How to Use Humor Correctly

Most people want to have a sense of humor or be around someone who does. So, how do you start adding a little more *Glee* to your *Me*? Don't be intimidated by humor. People appreciate a well-timed bit of humor to brighten up their day. But there are a few things to keep in mind:

* **Keep it clean.**

   Offensive language is never appropriate in the work-place—and you may not get invited back to the neighborhood barbeque if you use it there, either. Yes, people may laugh at a dirty joke, but it's probably more out of embarrassment. As my good friend Adam Christing, the founder of Clean Comedians, says, "It doesn't have to be filthy to be funny."

* **Keep it PC.**

   Yes, we live in the age of political correctness, and it's not going away. Racist, sexist, or suggestive humor is *never* appropriate. You don't know who might be offended by it, and it may come back to haunt you. Case in point: I once worked for a manager who was up for a promotion. When the woman with whom he was going to work found out this manager was being considered for the position, she informed their boss that he had used suggestive language on several occasions. Even though more than a year had passed since the incidents occurred, he was fired the next day. His co-worker had been offended and hadn't forgotten.

It seems like every week I hear of a new scandal involving some "leaked" internal videos from a highly regarded organization or individual. These private videos are meant to be funny but when revealed to the public they can be very offensive. They are certainly in bad taste and display poor judgment. Even if those involved try to explain the context—"We were just joking around!"—the damage is already done. The harm it does to their reputation or career can be irreparable.

* **Keep it brief.**

If you're going to tell a joke, don't tell long ones. As Shakespeare said, "Brevity is the soul of wit." A long joke is any joke that takes more than a minute to tell. If you're at the office, you're wasting valuable work time. And it's embarrassing for your audience to listen to a long joke and halfway through realize they've heard it before. Then they have to act like it was really funny, especially if it's the boss telling it. The exception for telling long jokes is when you're using them as a teaching tool to illustrate a point. Otherwise, I suggest using one-liners instead. I'll tell you where to find 'em at the end of this section.

* Too much of a good thing.

How do you know when there's too much humor in the workplace? When your humor turns into goofing off. Take yourself lightly and your work seriously.

* Get off the stage.

Nothing is more annoying than someone who is "always on." You can never get a straight answer from these people. It's as if they're always hiding something, and that's not good for building rapport or teamwork.

* Cut the sarcasm.

Sarcastic humor puts people on the defensive and creates a negative work environment. After a sarcastic comment, the person at whom it was directed has a natural urge to get even with a more cutting remark. Sure, you might find put-down humor funny—as long as the joke is not on you. And another thing, people who don't know you well might not know that you're kidding.

The same goes with teasing. Be extra careful with it. When I was a special education teacher I had an assistant who was cleaning up a very unpleasant mess. Me, wanting to be a team player, jumped right in to help, saying, "Hey, I can clean up messes too." He took it as an insult to his job responsibilities.

My intentions were make the best out of a bad situation using a little levity and showing what teamwork looks like; however, my attempt at humor was misinterpreted as a put-down and caused unnecessary tension in the workplace. A word to the wise: Never tease anyone who can bench press over 500 pounds!

Some people will never get your sense of humor, no matter how hard you try to convey it. Teasing will likely backfire, so don't push it. Instead, stay in the active mode and focus on how you can best meet the other person's needs at that time. Take into account that, as I mentioned earlier in the chapter, 5 percent of people are in a bad mood four out of every five days. Try not to make it five out of five for them.

Visual humor is often the most effective.

A good goal for all of us is to never have to ask the question, "Can't you take a joke?" We all know that many times the answer is "No!"

* **Let other things be funny for you.**

Visual humor is often the most effective. Share a funny cartoon with your co-workers, or put a humorous picture on the fridge for your family or roommates to enjoy. A little goes a long way. It shows them you have a good sense of humor. And if they don't think it's funny, no worries. It's not your joke anyway, so don't take it personally.

These are just a few simple parameters to help you become the funny guy/gal vs. the obnoxious one. Incorporating humor into your daily life can be really simple. Next we're going to talk about some places you can find humor.

Where's the Funny?

It may seem awkward to try using more humor in your life, so I'm going to give you some ideas on where to find it. It's pretty simple. You will be the king or queen of jocularity in no time!

There are many ways to add more humor to your life. I'm going to share with you some of my favorites. Not everything will work in every situation, so try the ones that fit your personal style. So here are a few tips for adding humor to everyday life as well as the workplace:

* **Personal stories.**

   Everyone has a funny story to tell. Think of something unusual or embarrassing that's happened to you and share it. Just make sure it's appropriate for the time and place.

* Practice, practice, practice.

   Find a couple of jokes or one-liners you are comfortable saying and practice them. Tell them to your friends. Find occasions to use them. Most comedians use some of the same jokes over and over, night after night, year after year—but they give you the *impression* they are telling them to you for the first time. It's strange, but the more you say them, the more "fresh" they sound. Of course, if you're always speaking to the same group, you won't want to be using the same jokes.

* **Take a trip down memory lane.**

Reminisce about things you did when you were a kid. It's always good for a laugh. For example, when I was a kid, I was allowed to ride in the front seat of the car. Actually, I was allowed to *stand* in the front seat of the car—without a seatbelt. I didn't need one; I had my mom's arm to hold me back in case of a sudden stop!

* **Watch and listen to children.**

We are all just "big" little kids. We basically have the same problems they do, only the seriousness of our situation has changed. We can learn so much about ourselves just by watching and listening to what children. They say and do the silliest things—and so do we.

* **"Do you ever…?"**

Use this intro to share some silly or absent-minded things you sometimes do. Example: Do you ever find yourself in another room looking for something and you forget what it is you are supposed to be looking for?

* **"You know what bugs me…?"**

Talk about annoying things that bother you, such as people who don't signal when they are making a turn and people who talk too loudly on their cell phones.

Make it fun. Even exaggerate a little. It's a great stress reliever. Wanna know what bugs me? Road construction. Traffic is backed up for miles. When you finally pass the site, you see 50 guys standing around watching one person work…and that one person working is the woman…holding up the sign that says, "Slow, men working!"

* **"You know you're getting older when…"**

Kid around about what it's like getting older. For instance, when I drop something on the floor, I wait until I drop something else so I don't have to make two trips!

* **Demonstrate how to do something by doing it incorrectly.**

If you need to teach people how to do something, start by showing them how *not* to do it. You can use humor to say something serious. You can get your point across without being heavy-handed.

* **Consult cartoon books.**

Find a book full of funny cartoons you can share. A few of my favorites are *Herman*, *The Far Side*, *Dilbert*, and *Ashleigh Brilliant*. There are plenty more. Just check out your local bookstore and find some you like. Many times I can tell the kind of stress people have in their lives by the cartoons they enjoy. Remember, conflict is one of the components of humor. They've identified the conflict, and they can relate to it. If you can laugh about it, you can talk about it.

* **Do the Hokey Pokey.**

I dare you not to laugh—or at least smile—while you're in a group doing the Hokey Pokey. It's a fun way to start or end a meeting.

* **Read or listen to something funny before a difficult task.**

Humor improves your problem-solving skills.[32] Laugh a little before you start, and you will find that you are smart!

* **Make sure there is someone in your life who can make you laugh.**

Life is tough. It's always nice to have that friend you can call and say, "I just need to laugh." My friends usually tell me to hold my facial cheeks up with tape and rubber bands.

* **Go to the corner drug store and read the funny greeting cards.**

It's a great mood-lifter, and it inspires you to be creative. While you're there, buy a funny greeting card and give it to a friend who could use a good laugh. You can also go to the bookstore and hang out in the humor section. You're sure to find a book or two that suits your great sense of humor.

---

32. Daniel Goleman, "Humor Found to Aid Problem-Solving," *New York Times*, August 4, Late Edition (east Coast). http://www.proquest.com.ezproxy.lapl.org/ accessed September 14, 2010.

* Remember the funny stuff you see and hear.

If you hear a funny line or see a funny message, write
it down so you'll remember it. I saw a bumper sticker
that said, "Attention carjackers. The car in front of
me is much nicer." I saw another bumper sticker that
said, "Don't laugh, it's paid for." It was on a brand new
Rolls-Royce! Okay, I made up the last part. It wasn't a
Rolls-Royce—it was a Ferrari!

* Introduce yourself in a funny way.

I met a man who had a patch over his eye. When he
introduced himself to me, he said, "Hello, my name
is Bill…with one 'i.'" I'm not making this story up. It
was a great way to break the ice and have a
little chuckle. When I make
cold calls, I say, "Hi, I'm Nick
Arnette, and I transform and
energize with humor. How
'bout that?" It always gets a
little laugh. You don't have to
go for a big laugh. Just a gesture
of humor sets a good tone for a
first impression.

Hello,
my name
is Bill…
with one 'i.'

* Find some good jokes online.

There are all kinds of great, free rib-ticklers online.
Just do a simple Internet search for the kind of jokes
you like—business jokes, one-liners, etc. There are lots
available. Of course, I highly recommend clean jokes,
especially if you plan on using the humor in a business
setting.

Using Humor in the Workplace

The ideas in the previous chapter for where to find humor will cross over for the workplace, but the following list is even more workplace specific. Remember, because of varied work environments and situations, not everything will work. Pick a couple that you like and give 'em a try.

* **Create a humor file.**

  When you come across something funny, save it. It can come in mighty handy at a later time.

* **Start meetings with a joke.**

  It's a great way to get people's attention and alleviate any tension that may be in the room.

* **Send team members on an office treasure hunt.**

  Hide a few goodies and gift cards around the office. Put some clues in office memos without telling anyone about it. You'll quickly find out who is reading your memos and who isn't. It's a fun way of saying, "Please read the office memos. They are valuable."

* **Make office memos fun.**

  Add at least one funny item to every memo. A funny quote or cartoon would be perfect.

* **Play the baby picture game.**

  Have everyone provide a baby photo and try to match photos with co-workers. Always good for a laugh.

* **Initiate theme days.**

  You might find your stress level going down and your creativity going up when you are in the theme of the day. Example: '60s day. Have you ever seen a stressed-out flower child?

* **Create a humor bulletin board.**

  Have a place to post funny pictures or articles. It can be a place to go to when you need a little giggle. Keep it fresh. Don't get caught with old jokes! You can vote on the best joke of the week.

* **Close the deal with humor.**

  If you're negotiating something, humor is a great way to break the ice. You get a feel for a person when you see how they respond to a little humor. It gives you a good idea how to handle the situation. If used properly, humor can be a very effective negotiating tool.[33] How do you think the phrase "you can catch more flies with honey than with vinegar" became an adage?

If used properly, humor can be a very effective negotiating tool.

* **Make up an office scapegoat.**

Make up a fictitious name of someone to blame things on when something goes wrong. You can get your message across quickly without accusing anyone directly. Example: "Looks like 'Nick Dude' forgot to let everyone know about the meeting on Friday."

* **Create a fun waiting area.**

If you have an office with a waiting room, leave some fun things for them to read, such as cartoon books, puzzle books, etc. It will put people in a better mood and make your job easier when it's time for them to see you.

* **Whistle while you work.**

Make the best of mundane tasks. Try to find a way to make them fun. When I was in the mortgage business we'd have end of the month loan processing pizza parties. We played

Put a picture of yourself as a kid on your desk.

---

33. John Forester, "Responding to Critical Moments with Humor, Recognition, and Hope," *Negotiation Journal*, 20 (2004) p. 2.

lively music, told lots of jokes, and ate lots of pizza. We had the mindset that we knew this wasn't fun, but let's make the best of it and get though it together.

* **Put a picture of yourself as a kid on your desk.**
It'll remind you of a time in your life when you didn't take yourself so seriously.

* **Write some of your own ideas to bring more humor to your work and home life:**

_____

_____

_____

_____

_____

_____

_____

_____

_____

_____

_____

_____

Using Humor in the Workplace

_____

_____

_____

_____

_____

_____

_____

_____

_____

_____

_____

_____

_____

_____

_____

_____

_____

Conclusion

Okay, class, time for the final exam: Each question is worth four points.

1. Most people fail when they forget to use the "basics."

   True   False

2. Your thoughts influence how you feel, how you feel affects how you behave, and how you behave over time determines your character.

   True   False

3. People are most likely to fail "in the moment."

   True   False

4. In the active mode, you are in charge of your own thoughts and actions.

   True   False

5. In the reactive mode, your response is based on how someone acts toward you.

   True   False

6. If the solution to a problem rests on what someone else should be doing, control of your life has gone out of your hands and into the hands of another person.

True   False

7. Everyone can learn to operate in the active mode.

True   False

8. Teamwork is a very vague concept.

True   False

9. Teamwork needs to be defined.

True   False

10. Teamwork does not come naturally in American society.

True   False

11. The key ingredient to teamwork is clear communication.

True   False

12. Every team should have a mission statement, and every team member should know what it is.

True   False

13. A team should be well aware of its strengths and weaknesses.

True   False

14. People on a team are working to accomplish a common purpose or goal, and all members are held mutually accountable for their contributions.

    True   False

15. The older we get, the less we laugh.

    True   False

16. Humor is an effective communication tool.

    True   False

17. Humor is a great quality in a leader.

    True   False

18. Humor is a great ice breaker and team builder.

    True   False

19. Humor can be used to say something serious.

    True   False

20. Sarcastic humor is counterproductive in the workplace.

    True   False

21. Humor can help ease stress.

    True   False

22. Humor is good for your mind and health.

    True   False

23. Humor is good for productivity.

    True   False

24. There's too much humor in the workplace if it turns into goofing off.

    True   False

25. Humor is a great morale booster.

    True   False

Bonus question (worth a million extra points):

26. You are glad you read this book!

    True   False

All right, let's see how you did. The answers for questions 1–25 are all true. I'm sure you all scored 100 points. Hopefully, the bonus question was true for you, too. In that case, your score is 1,000,100 points!

I hope you enjoyed your *Me We Glee* journey. It was a lot of fun sharing it with you.

Please remember that *Me*, *We*, and *Glee* all complement each other. Have all three and triumphant you'll be, I guarantee. I have to stop now because I don't have any more catchy rhymes.

The End

Bibliography

Arbell, Tali. "This & That," *Pittsburgh Post-Gazette*, November 12, http://www.proquest.com.ezproxy.lapl.org/ accessed September 9, 2010.

Arnetz, Bengt B.; Ekman, Rolf. *Stress in Health and Disease*, 1st edition, Wiley-VCH, 2006.

Casey, Aggie; Benson, Herbert; MacDonald, Ann. *Mind Your Heart: A Mind/Body Approach to Stress Management, Exercise, and Nutrition for Heart Health,* Simon and Shuster, 2004.

Daughters, Howard. "In Flight Humor." http://www.funny2.com/ inflight.htm accessed September 9, 2010.

Derfel, Aaron. "Deconstructing Stress," *The Gazette*, February 25, 2006. http://www.proquest.com.ezproxy.lapl.org/ accessed September 11, 2010.

Devries, Stephen. "Mind has effect on physical health," *Chicago Sun-Times*, February 28. http://www.proquest.com.ezproxy.lapl.org/ accessed September 11, 2010.

Forester, John. "Responding to Critical Moments with Humor, Recognition, and Hope," *Negotiation Journal*, 20 (2004) p. 2.

Garnett, James L.; Kouzmin, Alexander. *Handbook of Administrative Communication.*

Goleman, Daniel. "Humor Found to Aid Problem-Solving," *New York Times*, August 4, Late Edition (east Coast). http://www.proquest.com.ezproxy.lapl.org/ accessed September 14, 2010.

Hales, Dianne. *An Invitation to Health*, 6th edition, Cengage Learning, 2008.

Jensen, Eric. *Brain-Based Learning: The New Paradigm of Teaching.*

Lang, Susan S.; Patt, Richard B. *You Don't Have to Suffer: A Complete Guide to Relieving Cancer Pain for Patients and Their Families*, Oxford University Press, 1994.

Mori, Kazuo; Mori, Hideko. "Another Test of the Passive Facial Feedback Hypothesis: When Your Face Smiles, You Feel Happy,"

Perceptual and Motor Skills, 109, no. 1, (August), p. 76. http://www.proquest.com.ezproxy.lapl.org/ accessed September 2, 2010.

Park, Alice. "A Primer for Pessimists," *TIME*, March 26, 2009. http://www.time.com/time/magazine/article/0,9171,1887872,00.html accessed October 4, 2010.

Ritchie, Gayle. "Death by numbers: Start counting the cost of your bad habits," *The Daily Mirror*, January 13, 2010. http://www.proquest.com.ezproxy.lapl.org/ accessed September 11, 2010.

Rosato, Donna. "Putting humor to work in the workplace. Guest CEO: Herb Kelleher of Southwest Airlines" *USA TODAY*, February 23. http://www.proquest.com.ezproxy.lapl.org/ accessed September 4, 2010.

Ryan, Monique. "The Missing Ingredient?" *Outside*, June 2010. http://outsideonline.com/outside/bodywork/201006/vitamin-d-health-athletic-performance-tips.html accessed October 4, 2010.

Rynk, Peggy. "The value of a healthy attitude: how faith, anger, humor, and boredom can affect your health," *Vibrant Life*, March-April 2003. http://find.galegroup.com/gtx/start.do?prodId=ITOF&userGroupName=lapl accessed August 17, 2010.

Sauter, Steven L.; Murphy, Lawrence R.; Hurrell, Joseph J. Jr. "Prevention of Work-Related Psychological Disorders: A National Strategy Proposed by the National Institute for Occupational Safety and Health (NIOSH)." *The American Psychologist* 45, no. 10, October 1: 1146. http://www.proquest.com.ezproxy.lapl.org/ accessed September 11, 2010.

Smith, Susan A. "TV Makes You Smarter," *Psychology Today*, July 1, 2004. http://www.psychologytoday.com/articles/200410/tv-makes-you-smarter accessed October 23, 2010.

Strack, Fritz; Leonard, Martin L.; Stepper, Sabine. "Inhibiting and Facilitating Conditions of the Human Smile: A Nonobtrusive Test of the Facial Feedback Hypothesis," *Journal of Personality and Social Psychology*, May 1988, Vol. 54, Iss. 5, pp. 768-767.

Weintraub, Arlene. "Napping Your Way to the Top," *Business Week*, November 27, 2006. http://www.businessweek.com/magazine/content/06_48/b4011101.htm accessed October 4, 2010.

Williams, Debra. "Laughter is the best medicine," *Redlands Daily Facts*, October 7. http://www.proquest.com.ezproxy.lapl.org/ accessed September 2, 2010.

"STRESS...At Work," National Institute for Health and Safety (NIOSH). http://www.cdc.gov/niosh/docs/99-101/ accessed September 11, 2010.

"A nap a day makes doctors okay, Stanford study finds," Physician Business Week, November 21, 2006. http://www.proquest.com. ezproxy.lapl.org/ accessed August 23, 2010.

"Giggling? You've got to laugh." 2009. Daily Record, May 11, http:// www.proquest.com.ezproxy.lapl.org/ (accessed September 7, 2010).

"Grin and bear it; Laughing does a body good," The Patriot Ledger [LIVING WELL Edition], September 28, 2005. http://www. proquest.com.ezproxy.lapl.org/ accessed September 11, 2010.

"Study finds body's response to repetitive laughter is similar to the effect of repetitive exercise," NewsRx Health & Science, May 16, 2010, p. 78. http://www.proquest.com.ezproxy.lapl.org/ accessed September 3, 2010.

"Can blocking a frown keep bad feelings at bay?" Surgery Litigation & Law Weekly, University of Wisconsin-Madison, February 19, 2010, p. 1177. http://www.proquest.com.ezproxy.lapl. org/ accessed September 2, 2010.

Index

Be sure and check out Nick Arnette's
other book:

The Book of Dude

Available in a printed version and
most electronic book formats.

Nick Arnette
The Feel Good Funny Guy

Email: nick@nickarnette.com
Web: www.NickArnette.com
Facebook: www.facebook.com/nick.arnette
Facebook fan page:
   facebook.com/NickArnette.Comedian
Twitter: @NickArnette, #MeWeGlee
Youtube: Nick Arnette's Channel

Me, We and Glee is also available in Kindle, Nook, Ibooks and most other ebook formats.

CPSIA information can be obtained
at www.ICGtesting.com
Printed in the USA
BVHW071725211021
619503BV00004B/12